Published in the German language originally under the title: Hilf dem Löwen Zähne putzen!
Boje Verlag in the Bastei Luebbe AG
© 2020 by Bastei Luebbe AG, Koeln, Germany.
ISBN 978-3-41482-561-2
Written by Sophie Schoenwald.
Illustrated by Günther Jakobs.

All rights reserved. No part of this book may be reproduced in any form without written permission from the publisher.

Copyright of the English edition by Evergreen Books.
Evergreen Books and freshabooks are imprints of:
freshamedia GmbH, Robert-Bosch-Straße 32 A, 63303 Dreieich, Germany.
English language translation copyright © Rachel Ward, 2021.

ISBN 978-3-96326-000-1

www.evergreen-books.de
www.help-the-lion.com

There's something wrong with Mr. Lion. Nobody has seen him in a long time – he must be hiding.

Can you find him?

Well done. There he is!
But why is he covering his mouth?

Tickle him behind the ears!
That'll make him laugh and show his teeth.

Ewww! What a stink!
Quick! Hold your nose!
It looks like it's been a while since
Mr. Lion brushed his teeth.
We're going to need a lot of help!

Beat the drum to call his friends
so you can help Mr. Lion together.

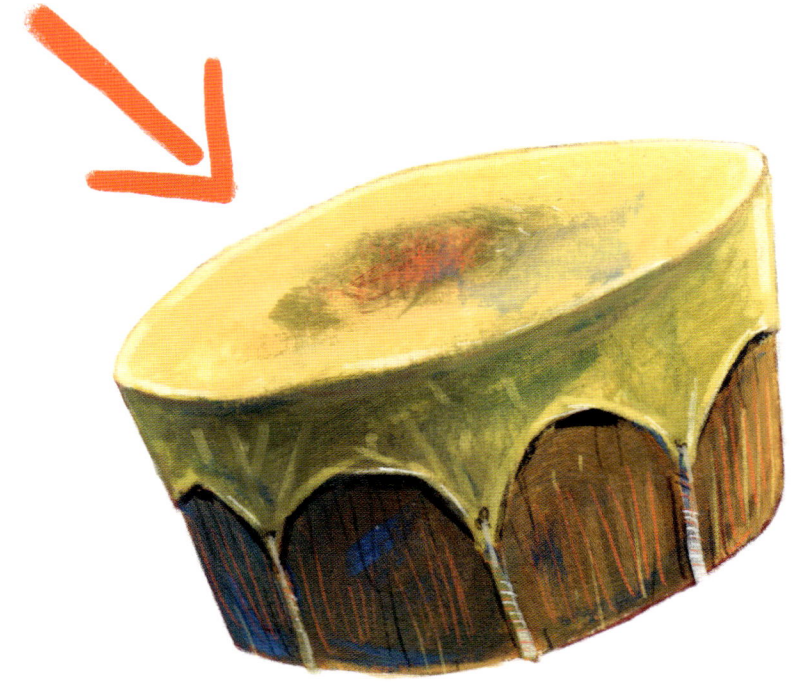

Great, they're all here!
Look, the little hedgehog has brought toothpaste.
Mr. Lion is very excited.
We need to calm him down.

Give his mane a stroke
before we get started.

Because Mr. Lion is very big and he has a lot of teeth, he needs an awful lot more toothpaste than you do.

So shut the book up nice and tight,
and give the tube a good squeeze!

Look, the toothpaste has landed
on the little hedgehog's bristly head.
Now you can get to work!

Scrub the chewing surfaces of Mr. Lion's back teeth.
Start on one side.
Do the top teeth first, then the bottom ones.
And then just the same on the other side.
Top teeth first, then the bottom ones.

Great!
Now it's time for the fronts.

Make big circles! Start in the middle and then work your way out.

That wasn't bad, but we can do even better.

Don't give up now. Keep on brushing!

Fantastic!
You've finished the fronts.
Mr. Lion deserves a little rest.

Pull the elephant's trunk
to fill the glass with water.
Then Mr. Lion and you can gargle together.

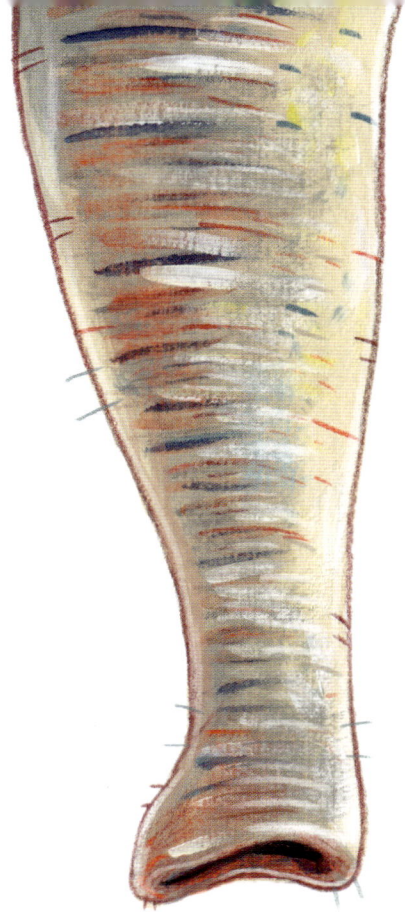

Great!

Now you're ready for the second half!

All we have to do now is scrub the backs.

Move from pink gums to white teeth.

The little hedgehog has a saying for remembering that:

"Always move from flamingo to polar bear."

So off you go!

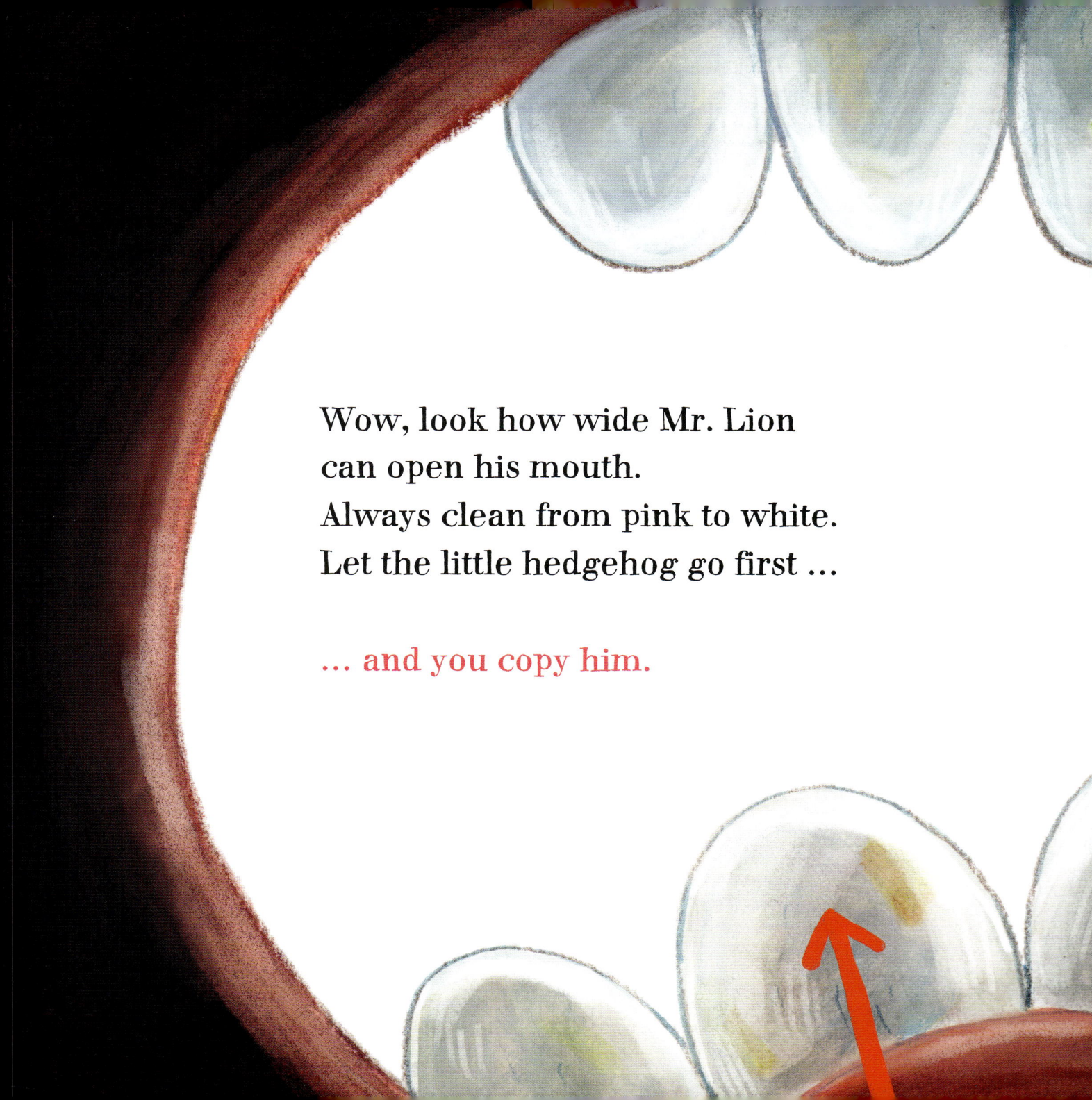

Wow, look how wide Mr. Lion
can open his mouth.
Always clean from pink to white.
Let the little hedgehog go first ...

... and you copy him.

We did it!
Mr. Lion can show off his brightest grin.
He wants to say thank you – look,
he's holding up his paw.

Give him a high five and
show him your best smile.

Now it's your turn.
Let Mom and Dad help you, and together
you'll get your teeth all shiny and clean.

There is more to discover from Evergreen Books!

A hare and a hedgehog become friends, respecting and enjoying what makes each of them unique. We learn that conflict in a friendship is okay, and can be overcome with love.

In a story celebrating parental love, a little monkey sets off to find the world's greatest treasure for his Mommy. After much adventuring, Mommy shows her child what means more to her than anything in the world.

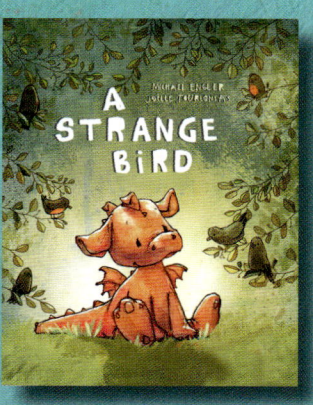

A Strange Bird is a heart-felt story about a baby dragon who can't seem to fit in - but refuses to give up. Ultimately, the dragon saves the day by daring to be different.